MLB's Greatest Teams

CINCINNATI REDS

Big Buddy Books

An Imprint of Abdo Publishing
abdopublishing.com

Katie Lajiness

abdopublishing.com

Published by Abdo Publishing, a division of ABDO, PO Box 398166, Minneapolis, Minnesota 55439.
Copyright © 2019 by Abdo Consulting Group, Inc. International copyrights reserved in all countries. No part
of this book may be reproduced in any form without written permission from the publisher. Big Buddy Books™
is a trademark and logo of Abdo Publishing.

Printed in the United States of America, North Mankato, Minnesota.
052018
092018

THIS BOOK CONTAINS
RECYCLED MATERIALS

Cover Photo: Andy Lyons/Getty Images.
Interior Photos: 33ft/Depositphotos (p. 7); Andy Lyons/Getty Images (pp. 5, 9); AP Images (pp. 13, 17, 19, 22,
    23, 28); Christian Petersen/Getty Images (p. 24); Everett Collection Inc/Alamy Stock Photo (p. 11); HC/
    AP Images (p. 15); Jennifer Stewart/Getty Images (pp. 25, 27); John Grieshop/Getty Images (p. 29); Marc
    Serota/Getty Images (p. 23); Rich Pilling/Getty Images (p. 25); Rick Stewart/Getty Images (p. 21).

Coordinating Series Editor: Tamara L. Britton
Graphic Design: Jenny Christensen

Library of Congress Control Number: 2017962671

Publisher's Cataloging-in-Publication Data

Names: Lajiness, Katie, author.
Title: Cincinnati Reds / by Katie Lajiness.
Description: Minneapolis, Minnesota : Abdo Publishing, 2019. | Series: MLB's greatest
    teams | Includes online resources and index.
Identifiers: ISBN 9781532115165 (lib.bdg.) | ISBN 9781532155888 (ebook)
Subjects: LCSH: Major League Baseball (Organization)--Juvenile literature. | Baseball
    teams--United States--History--Juvenile literature. | Cincinnati Reds (Baseball team)-
    -Juvenile literature. | Sports teams--Juvenile literature.
Classification: DDC 796.35764--dc23

Contents

Major League Baseball

League Play

There are two leagues in MLB. They are the American League (AL) and the National League (NL). Each league has 15 teams and is split into three divisions. They are east, central, and west.

The Cincinnati Reds is one of 30 Major League Baseball (MLB) teams. The team plays in the National League Central **Division**.

Throughout the season, each MLB team plays 162 games. The season begins in April and can continue until November.

Mr. Red is the Cincinnati Reds' oldest mascot. He joined the team in 1955!

A Winning Team

The Reds team is from Cincinnati, Ohio. The team's colors are red, white, and black.

The team has had good seasons and bad. But time and again, the Reds players have proven themselves. Let's see what makes the Reds one of MLB's greatest teams!

Fast Facts

HOME FIELD: Great American Ball Park

TEAM COLORS: Red, white, and black

TEAM SONG: "All I Do is Win" by DJ Khaled

PENNANTS: 10

WORLD SERIES TITLES: 1919, 1940, 1975, 1976, 1990

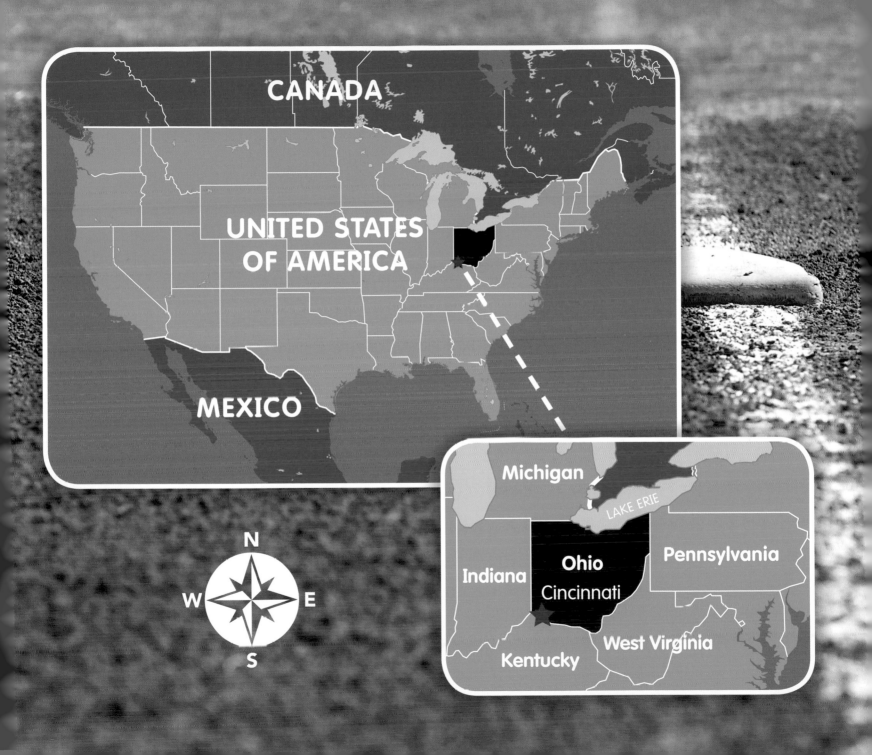

CANADA

UNITED STATES
OF AMERICA

MEXICO

N

W E

S

Michigan

LAKE ERIE

Indiana

Ohio

Pennsylvania

Cincinnati

West Virginia

Kentucky

Great American Ball Park

Union Grounds was the Reds' first ballpark. Its grandstand could hold only 4,000 people. The team played at this location from 1869 to 1870. After that, the Reds played on five different fields throughout Cincinnati.

In 2003, the Reds moved into the Great American Ball Park. It is located near the Ohio River in downtown Cincinnati. There, more than 42,000 people can watch the Reds play baseball.

The Great American Ball Park cost $280 million to build.

Then and Now

The Cincinnati Reds was America's first **professional** baseball team. It was founded in 1869 as the Red Stockings. In 1890, the team joined the NL along with seven other teams.

The Reds' name has been around since 1890. But before that, the team had different names. Those names include the Red Stockings and the Redlegs. Some even called it The Big Red Machine when it ruled the league in the 1970s.

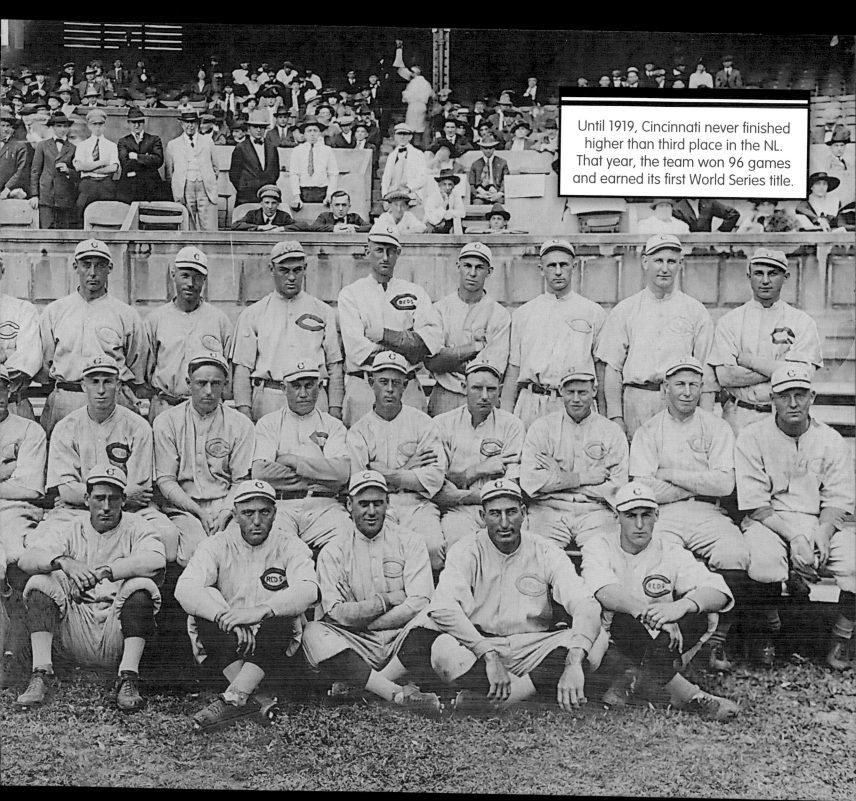

Until 1919, Cincinnati never finished higher than third place in the NL. That year, the team won 96 games and earned its first World Series title.

Cincinnati is a team of firsts. In 1935, it played the first night game in MLB history. President Franklin D. Roosevelt pressed a **telegraph** key from the White House in Washington, DC. That sent a signal to the Reds' president to flip a switch powering the lights.

In 1939, the team won an NL **pennant**. One year later, it earned a World Series title. But by the mid-1940s, the Reds often finished in the bottom half of the league. It would be more than 35 years until the team won another **championship**.

The Reds played the Detroit Tigers in the 1940
World Series. In Game Three, Bill Baker (*left*)
ran from second base to home on a single.

Highlights

The Reds enjoyed one of its best years in 1975. The Big Red Machine finished the regular season with 108 wins. And the team was first in the league for having the most runs.

Despite some struggles, the Reds have earned nine NL **pennants**. And, the team has won World Series titles in 1919, 1940, 1975, 1976, and 1990. It is one of eight teams to have won at least five World Series.

The Reds played the Boston Red Sox in the 1975 World Series. Cincinnati won four out of seven games to earn the title.

Win or Go Home

The top team from each AL and NL division goes to the playoffs. Each league also sends one wild-card team. One team from the AL and one from the NL will win the pennant. The two pennant winners then go to the World Series!

Over the years, the Reds team has earned many exciting records. Some team members are in the National Baseball Hall of Fame. Others have received spots as MLB's **Most Valuable Players (MVPs)**. And quite a few members have played in All-Star Games.

Pete Rose played for Cincinnati from the 1960s to the 1980s. He has won many of the most meaningful awards in MLB. That includes the 1975 World Series MVP Award.

Famous Managers

George Lee "Sparky" Anderson managed the Reds from 1970 to 1978. He led the Reds to NL **pennant** wins in 1970 and 1972.

Anderson helped the team earn the NL West title in 1973. Then the Reds won back-to-back World Series titles in 1975 and 1976.

Many believe that Anderson was the most successful manager in the team's history. He was **inducted** into the National Baseball Hall of Fame in 2000.

Sparky was the first manager to win championships in both the National and American leagues.

Lou Piniella managed the Reds from 1990 to 1992. While only with the team for three seasons, he was very successful. He led the team to the 1990 World Series. During his **career**, he coached the team to a 255-win record.

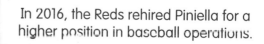

In 2016, the Reds rehired Piniella for a higher position in baseball operations.

Star Players

Tony Pérez FIRST BASEMAN, #24

Tony Pérez is said to be the heart and soul of the 1970s Reds team. He played for Cincinnati for 13 seasons. During this time, he helped the team win two World Series titles. In 2000, the Reds **retired** jersey number 24 to honor Pérez. That same year, he was **inducted** into the National Baseball Hall of Fame.

1964 – 1976

Johnny Bench CATCHER, #5

Johnny Bench played for the Cincinnati Reds for 17 years. During that time, he was the starting catcher for ten All-Star Games. Bench helped the Reds win two World Series. And, he hit an amazing 389 homers while with the team. Bench was inducted into the National Baseball Hall of Fame in 1989.

1967 – 1983

Joe Morgan SECOND BASEMAN, #8

Joe Morgan's second-base skills helped the Reds win two World Series titles. His accomplishments were honored with five **Gold Glove Awards**. Morgan joined the National Baseball Hall of Fame in 1990. Eight years later, the Reds **retired** jersey number 8 in his honor.

1972 – 1979

Ken Griffey Jr. CENTER FIELDER, #24

2000 – 2008

Ken Griffey Jr. was a baseball hero. He played with the Cincinnati Reds from 2000 to 2008. Throughout his MLB **career**, he earned two **MVP** Awards and ten Gold Glove Awards. And, he hit a whopping 630 home runs in 22 years! Griffey Jr. was **inducted** into the National Baseball Hall of Fame in 2016.

Joey Votto FIRST BASEMAN, #19

Joey Votto joined the Reds in 2007. He has proven to be a loyal player. In 2013 and 2017, Votto played in all 162 games of the season. For his efforts, Votto earned the 2010 NL **MVP** Award. The same year, he won the NL Hank Aaron Award for best batter in the league.

2007 –

Adam Duvall FIRST BASEMAN, #23

After joining the team, it was clear that Adam Duvall was a talented player. With 33 home runs in 2016, Duvall ranked sixth in the league for homers. That same year, he ranked fifth in the league for **runs batted in (RBIs)**. And in 2017, he played in all but five regular season games.

2015 –

Scooter Gennett SECOND BASEMAN, #4

Scooter Gennett joined the Reds for the 2017 season. His main position is second base. But in 2017, he also played third base, left field, and right field. That same year, he hit 27 home runs. He hit four of those homers in just one game!

2017 –

Raisel Iglesias PITCHER, #26

Raisel Iglesias began his baseball **career** in Cuba. **Recruiters** saw Iglesias throw a fastball at 97 miles (156 km) per hour! Soon after, the pitcher signed with the Cincinnati Reds. In 2017, Iglesias threw consistent pitches at 96 miles (155 km) per hour. As of 2017, Iglesias is the Reds' star closing pitcher.

2017 –

Final Call

The Cincinnati Reds have a long, rich history. The team has played in nine World Series and won five titles.

Even during losing seasons, true fans have stuck by the team. Many believe the Reds will remain one of the greatest teams in MLB.

All-Stars

The best players from both leagues come together each year for the All-Star Game. This game does not count toward the regular season records. It is simply to celebrate the best players in MLB.

At the end of the 2017 season, Joey Votto hit his thirty-fourth double. That means that after hitting a pitch, he made it safely to second base. And, he set a new Cincinnati Reds record.

Through the Years

1869

The Red Stockings finished its first **professional** baseball season. The team earned a perfect record of 57 wins and zero losses.

1919

The team won its first World Series in Game Eight against the Chicago White Sox.

1944

The youngest pitcher to appear in MLB played his first game. Joe Nuxhall was only 15 years old.

1956

The Reds set a new record by hitting eight homers in one game.

1967

The Reds played the longest game in team history. It lasted 21 innings.

1984

Former Reds outfielder Pete Rose became the team's new manager.

1990

The team held on to its spot in first place for the entire regular season. It was the first team in the NL to do so.

2003

Cincinnati hosts the season opener in its brand-new Great American Ball Park.

2012

The Reds won 97 games, earning the team its second NL Central title in three seasons.

Glossary

career a period of time spent in a certain job.

championship a game, a match, or a race held to find a first-place winner.

division a number of teams grouped together in a sport for competitive purposes.

Gold Glove Award annually given to the MLB players with the best fielding experience.

induct to officially introduce someone as a member.

Most Valuable Player (MVP) the player who contributes the most to his or her team's success.

pennant the prize that is awarded to the champions of the two MLB leagues each year.

professional (pruh-FEHSH-nuhl) working for money rather than only for pleasure.

recruiter a person who finds members to join a team.

retire to withdraw from use or service.

run batted in (RBI) a run that is scored as a result of a batter's hit, walk, or stolen base.

telegraph a machine used to send messages across wires.

Online Resources

Booklinks
NONFICTION NETWORK
FREE! ONLINE NONFICTION RESOURCES

To learn more about the Cincinnati Reds, visit **abdobooklinks.com**. These links are routinely monitored and updated to provide the most current information available.

Index